Jack: Are you ready to go o the tour?

Giants: Yes, we are!

Jack: Please be sure not to tread on me!

Mum: Did you hear that, Midge?

Midge: Yes, Mum.

Jack and the Giants
A Play

The Characters

Mum
Dad   } *three giant tourists*
Midge

Jack   *a tour guide*

Jack: Hello, giants. I'm Jack, and I'm going to show you round the town.

Mum: Hello, Jack!

Dad: Hello, Jack!

Midge: He is so cute!

Jack: Off we go then! Follow me, please, giants.

Dad: What a cute little village!

Jack: It's not a village. It's a huge town!

Mum: Look at that cute little ribbon.

Jack: It's not a ribbon. It's a river!

Midge: Look at that cute little bridge!
Can I put it in my fish tank?

Mum: No, you can't.

Jack: Now, this is the art gallery.

Dad: Look at those cute little stamps!

Jack: They are not stamps. They are big pictures!

Midge: Can I put them in my doll's house?

Dad: No, you can't.

Jack: Now, this is the zoo.

Midge: Look at that cute little kitten!

Jack: It's not a kitten. It's a huge tiger!

Mum: Look at that cute little creature with the thin little neck!

Jack: That's a giraffe!

Midge: Is there a gift shop, Dad?

Dad: I don't know. Let's ask Jack.

Mum: Where is Jack?

Dad: Yes, where is he?

Mum: I hope you didn't tread on him, Midge.

Jack: Let me out! Let me out!

Dad: I can hear his cute little voice!

Jack: Let me out!

Mum: It's coming from your pocket, Midge.

Jack: Put me down!

Dad: Yes, put him down, Midge!

Midge: But I want to take him back and put him in my doll's house.

Mum: Well you can't.

Jack: The tour is over!